MANIFESTATION MASTERY

MANIFESTATION MASTERY

How to Work with the Quantum Field and Hack the Matrix

By Jen McCarty

REVIEWS FOR MANIFESTATION MASTERY

"Dear reader, whether you are being introduced to Jen and her work for the first time or are an avid follower of Jen's teachings', you will find within a beautiful map that will take you on a most extraordinary journey bringing you to where you have chosen to arrive.

You will be shown clearly every turn toward your every desire, and you will find along the way it is already alive and living.

If you follow the precise direction within this map, you will be shown places in yourself you have never been before and the help to navigate your destination even when you can't see.

*By journeys end you will be masterfully manifesting your desires as you travel a most exquisite journey into yourself." ~**Sheila F.***

"The information contained in this book has the direct impact to change your life to what so many dream about for themselves and what your soul longs for.

Jens gained and acquired the golden nuggets to fast track your life to one of love, fulfilment, harmony, and abundance.

*This is a book for those that know your soul is calling you to become more of who you truly are, that it's an inside job and only you can do it for yourself." ~**Daniel S – Certified Life Coach***

*"Jen McCarty's words and codes come through the pages with such a deep desire to assist all of us in such a way that every soul will feel the shifts and experience and manifest abundance in all areas. This can come in with synchronicities, aha moments, material manifestation, in bite size packs, or in leaps and bounds. It is all up to each of us individually in the end. This book is to help all of us experience this magical Universe we live in! A must read!" ~**Teri-Lee***

Proofreading and Front/Back Matter Copy Editing: Zoe Gaunt

zoeyg@protonmail.com

Book Front Cover Artist: Jen McCarty

First Print Edition 21/12/2021

ISBN: 9798831870046

Disclaimer Notice:

Although the author has made every effort to ensure that the information in this book was correct at time of press, the author does not assume and hereby disclaims any liability to any party for any loss, damage, or disruption caused by errors or omissions, whether such errors or omissions result from negligence, accident, or any other cause.

This book is not intended as a substitute for the medical advice of physicians. The reader should regularly consult a physician in matters relating to his/her health and particularly with respect to any symptoms that may require diagnosis or medical attention.

All of the information that I share has been received directly through my own access to the Akashic Records. Nothing that I share is regurgitated information; it is all based on downloads that I have personally received. It is so important that as you are reading these words, you exercise your own discernment and only take on as truth that which resonates for you as truth. If something does not feel true to you, then that is correct; so please do honour that.

Regardless of where you are on your spiritual path, whether you be a beginner or a seasoned explorer into the deepest mysteries of existence, the words in this book will awaken memories in you that have long been sleeping - memories of your true and abiding divinity.

The words are organised in such a way that it can be likened to light language and light codes. These words transcend the boundaries of time and space and align immediately with your heart's consciousness. The key to Christ Consciousness is through the heart.

In love and eternal light, Jen and the White Wolf Tribe.

DEDICATION

I dedicate this book
to the God-Flame that exists in all.

PUBLISHED BY:

Blue Flame 5D Media

ACKNOWLEDGEMENTS

As we know, creating a book requires a team and I would like to now acknowledge all of the beautiful souls that have contributed to this powerful and sacred manual.

I would like to thank all the members of Team Jen; Zoe, Gurpreet and Eddie. You are my dream team and without you, this book would never have been created.

I would like to honour Zoe for proofreading the document and for her help in formatting the book and structuring the chapters and doing all the back pages and front pages and assisting me with the layout of the book.

I would like to thank my personal assistants Gurpreet and Zoe for being the best personal assistants you could ever pray for.

I would like to acknowledge the mentors that have inspired me to create this book, Neville Goddard and T. Harv Eker and all of the Ascended beings that I work with so closely. All of you have inspired me so deeply and I acknowledge you for all the inspiration that I've received from you.

I would also like to acknowledge my beautiful son for continuing to be my greatest spiritual teacher and always teaching me about forgiveness and that the true spiritual master is able to forgive easily.

I would like to thank my large spiritual community for all of their love and support and for all the members of the Street Team that have read the book prior to its publication.

And thank you to my Divine Oversoul for all the wisdom I have been so blessed to receive in this lifetime.

TABLE OF CONTENTS

INTRODUCTION

Manifestation Mastery Book – Section One

It is my deepest honour to welcome you on this powerful journey of transformation and enlightenment.

This is the third book that I have created, and I am so delighted to share with you some of the most incredible codes that will enable you to become a master manifestor.

In this powerful manual, I will share with you all that I have learned about manifestation in the last 25 years and beyond, since my third eye blasted open, and the veil to higher consciousness was opened and all multi-dimensional celestial glory was revealed to me.

What I know primarily, is that this is a vibrational universe, and we all live and coexist within a vast quantum field.

This means that there are an infinite number of possibilities, that are available to us in every single moment, and we as God beings, have the power to choose and attune our thoughts, frequency, and embodiment to the vibration of that which we wish to experience in order to magnetise it into our reality.

We are extremely powerful, multi-dimensional Avatar transmitters, and throughout our existence there have been multiple attempts to hijack our consciousness by the old controllers of the matrix. But the greatest power in the universe is accessed by our awakening and remembrance of the truth that we are all divine children of God.

In the moment, whereby we truly awaken to our divinity and our multi-dimensionality, we fully and completely remember that all that truly exists is the eternal moment of now. The matrix programming has sought to entrain and indoctrinate everyone to believe that time is somewhat linear, but nothing could be further from the truth.

Time, if anything is vertical as all timelines run concurrently within the present moment of now. Therefore, our duty as God's innocent eternal offspring is to arrive home, anchored in the present moment with the knowing and remembrance that the present moment is our eternal resting place, and is the place our soul has been seeking for eternity.

Manifestation Mastery Oracle Deck

Whilst writing this sacred manual - Manifestation Mastery, I was deeply guided to share with everybody the light codes that I have created as an oracle deck in order to support in the opening and expansion to receive the powerful, sacred reminder codes in this book.

The codes are inspired by my galactic connections to the Pleiades, and if people ask me, I will say they are inspired by my Pleiadian galactic lineage.

It is very unusual when we encounter a deck of oracle cards to meet cards that were created artistically by the author and creator of the deck, because of this, this adds a particular potency and alignment with the frequency, the messages of these cards.

There are so many ways that you can work with these cards.

They truly are a blessing from above. There is an option for you to be able to purchase the oracle deck cards at the back of this book so that you are able to work with them to inspire your healing and alignment with your higher-self.

These cards were created with the utmost devotion and love and the desire to serve my brothers and sisters and eternally remind them of their connection within - their own self to eternal source energy.

Please remember that in order to experience true and lasting healing on the spiritual path, you must find and commit to a spiritual practice that will bring you home to the zero-point field / the present moment where all timelines converge into the present moment of now.

Therefore, each of the oracle cards include instructions on how to work with each of the light codes contained within the deck, plus you also have the option to purchase the MP3 Activation which will greatly assist you with absorbing the codes and creating and committing to a spiritual practice.

That must be the priority, bringing our awareness to the place where all timelines collapse into presence, remembering to always in this moment show up as the I Am presence that "I Am that I Am."

All of the words in the book, all of the intention behind the creation of the cards, and all of the codes in the messages of the cards are infused with a sacred desire for you to awaken proficiently and swiftly to the truth of your eternal and perpetual innocence as a divine child of eternal love.

What a great and wondrous journey we have been on. How brave you are to have returned back to this earthly plane at this time, and how inspired it is that you were vibrationally drawn to these extremely blessed and transformative oracle cards.

May you allow the love of your higher-self to permeate through your crown center, into your heart, to activate your thymus gland, the seat of unconditional love, that you may awaken to the love that our creator has for you.

In that awakening, may you awaken to your duty to love your brothers and sisters in the way that creator loves you.

It is always my deepest honour to serve my brothers and sisters, and I deeply look forward to bringing through this oracle deck in order to assist you with returning home to the zero-point field.

Please enjoy these sacred codes.

Take them deep into your heart and allow them to permeate with your DNA strands to activate the codes of coherence after that long time scramble since the fall of Atlantis.

We are the ones that we have been praying for.

We are the ones that we have been waiting for.

There is no saviour out there who is coming to save you.

Thank God you are the saviour of your own very self, for you are a sovereign soul.

You are a sovereign being.

It is time now to wear your crown with pride, that all your lost and asleep brothers and sisters may be given an opportunity to remember their heritage and their eternal divinity.

The Oracle card deck will deeply support you on your journey of becoming a more master manifestor. I highly recommend that you work with these cards. The cards are encoded with light symbols that I have channelled, that will deeply enable you to transform your consciousness and upgrade your consciousness to the fifth-dimension or Christ consciousness.

In love and eternal light, Jen and the White Wolf Tribe.

"From Abundance he took and still Abundance remains"

—UPANISHADS

CHAPTER 1

AWAKENING TO OUR DIVINITY

We understand that it is our anchoring in the present moment, which truly is the greatest gift that our higher self, our creator self, has given us in every single moment. So therefore, when we come home to the zero-point field also known as the present moment, we understand that in each moment we are presented with a choice - to love or to fear, to choose to create or to be in victim mode.

These are essentially the two choice points we are presented with in every single moment. Because of the obsession of the third-dimensional prison matrix structure, many of us have forgotten that indeed we are endowed with the power to co-create our reality, and to choose and attune to whatever timeline we wish to, in any and every single moment.

And beyond that, we actually have a duty to do that, especially if we are one of the 144,000. We made a promise to all of our brothers and sisters that truly we would awaken and remember this ancient, absolute truth.

There is nothing outside of yourself that your soul is seeking. Happiness and the direct knowing and experience of your Christ self, the eternal higher self, the divine self, the innocent childlike self, dwells within all of us. We each hold the Trinity, the mother self, the father self and the child self, the divine mother, the divine father, and the Christ Sophia child. I am that I am.

On the path to abiding spiritual awakening and manifestation mastery, we remember that it is our absolute duty to step forward and protect and nurture the sacred eternal child self that dwells within. We remember that our eternal child self is deeply and intricately wedded to God's heart throughout eternity.

As one truly, truly awakens to their divinity and comes home to the present moment, it becomes obviously clear that we live in a multi-dimensional universe. And in that multi-dimensional universe, we have access to every single thing our hearts desire.

At this point, it would be extremely pertinent to remind ourselves that our hearts desires are specifically handpicked and blueprinted by the divine in us at the moment of our birth. Our desires are encoded within our heart matrix ready to be activated at the exact perfect moment on our timeline destiny.

CHAPTER 2

THE HOLINESS OF OUR DESIRES

Our desires are indeed extremely holy. The desire to serve, the desire to be in a sacred union, the desire to be a wonderful mother and father, the desire to be an extremely wealthy and abundant soul, the desire to manifest a particular specific vehicle. All of these desires are holy desires that are specifically placed within our soul, and they are definitely not random.

We must remember that there has been an agenda to attempt to cast a shadow over these most sacred inner knowing's that we all carry, And a societal programming which has sought to belittle and diminish the importance of the sacred desires of our heart……

It is very important on the path of manifestation mastery to become a 100% committed rebel to all third-dimensional limited programming. In order to access and activate the quantum realms you have to drop your victim story and remember that you are casting spells in every single moment that you speak.

It is your absolute duty to take full responsibility for the spells that you cast because as you are speaking, you are creating the world and reality that you wish to experience.

As a master manifestor, we understand that all quantum timelines exist.

It is very important for all of you who are reading these words to remember that there is a very powerful string that attaches us to every single one of our hearts and souls desires. And in order for us to experience those desires, we have to vibrate at the frequency of those desires.

But the big question is how do we do that?

One of the ways that we do that is we talk ourselves into that way of being, we speak to ourselves as though we have arrived at that place already!!

We create visual images and representations in the present moment of now, which show us that we are living in this vibration right now.

We set a goal: for example, if you wish to manifest a hundred thousand pounds income per month, you say to the universe, "This is my intention." Then you understand that we live in a quantum universe, and you reach into the quantum realm to connect and empower that string that connects you to this specific heart's desire.

You deeply act as if it has already manifested, and you empower the reality that this has already happened. This way you deeply connect with the string in the quantum realm, and your consciousness weaves deeply into that string (where that reality is already being experienced) this is when miracles happen.

I always highly recommend working with techniques such as this the moment we wake up in the morning and just before we go to sleep at night. When we work in this particular state of consciousness between waking and sleeping, the veil between our subconscious mind is extremely non-existent which enables the instructions from our heart to go directly into our subconscious mind without any resistance.

This is a fundamental aspect of manifestation which if taken onboard will produce life-changing results very, very quickly.

CHAPTER 3

AN INTRODUCTION TO THE QUANTUM FIELD

One of the fastest ways to transform your vibration in the quantum realm and generally transform your capacity to be able to hold greater and greater levels of wealth, abundance and love in the quantum field is to connect with mentors, coaches, teachers, guides that have reached the level you wish to attain- be that wealth/ income, be that relationship success or be that someone who has reached a level of spiritual mastery that you wish to attain.

Spending time around mentors that have calibrated to a high level of mastery, is an extremely fast way for us to fast track our own up levelling and is highly recommended on the path to manifestation mastery.

When you are truly clear about what your heart desires to manifest, it's very important you show up in the world as he or she who's living that as a reality. If you wish to manifest a sacred relationship with an extremely successful and wealthy partner that you are deeply connected to on a soul level, show up in the world as she who has already achieved that. Wear gorgeous clothes, manifest the self-love. Choose to show up in that classy way, as you would, as she.

Scripting

I would like to devote the next few paragraphs to speaking about a very, very powerful manifestation technique called scripting. Scripting is when we take a piece of paper and write out in the present tense exactly what our life looks like as if we are directly experiencing that which we wish to manifest - that which we wish to experience on the third-dimensional plane.

When we script we go into as much detail as we possibly can, to imprint upon our subconscious mind the fact that this truly is happening.

Indeed, this is entirely what the whole journey of manifestation ultimately comes down to. And that is that we must Imprint upon our subconscious mind the successful manifestation of all our hearts desires.

We must remember that our desires are beautiful, sacred, exotic flowers that are growing in the garden of our hearts. But around these sacred, beautiful flowers, there are many, many weeds representing all the false beliefs and programs of the generations that have come before us (as well as the societal matrix), which questions and devalues these precious desires, and makes us question their sacredness.

It is important, if you wish for these desires of your heart to flourish, that you weed out all beliefs and all thoughts of doubt that are preventing, blocking, and disabling these beautiful, sacred, exotic flowers of the desires of your heart to grow.

This is one of the most potent manifestation principles and practises that if applied, will produce the most extraordinarily phenomenal results in your reality.

Sacred Exercise

In order to experience scripting, please take out a large sheet of paper and choose one of your dreams, one of your goals that you would like to achieve.

Please write out a future date and start writing out in diary form as though that which you wish to create has already manifested.

For example, if you wish to manifest earning £100,000 per month income, you could write something like this.

"Wow, it was so amazing. I set a goal to achieve £100,000 a month and within three weeks, I achieved it. I didn't have to work any harder. In fact, I worked less on my business. I simply understood and deeply respected the desire of my heart to level up to this income level. I held the faith and I created offers that would enable me to hit that target. But then I absolutely let go.

I contacted the higher self of my soulmate clients and let them know that I was available to serve them. I put zero energy into hustle, and I put all my energy into alignment. I worked with the quantum field to align with the brothers and sisters, who I had made a soul contract to work with. They all found me, and I easily achieved my £100,000 a month."

This is a perfect example to illustrate how to work with the power of scripting. Your subconscious mind does not know the difference between that which you imagine, and that which is real, so informing your subconscious mind in this manner is extremely potent, and life changing and extremely powerful.

I highly recommend applying the principle of scripting to all areas of your life, to all aspects of your life that you wish to up level and indeed manifest. Some of the most inspiring manifestors that I work with all use this scripting method. I have seen people manifest their Twin Flame, their ideal location to live in, and their ideal income purely from scripting it. I really and absolutely cannot stress the power of working with this manifestation technique.

"When you want something the whole universe will conspire for you to have it"

—PAULO COHELLO

CHAPTER 4

SHADOW WORK AND MANIFESTATION

Understanding and identifying the shadow aspect is a fundamental part of manifestation and is deeply connected to showing up for yourself and vigilantly always doing the soul retrieval work. This is a subject matter which hardly anyone actually really speaks about in the manifestation world. But shadow work is an absolutely fundamental aspect of becoming a master manifestor.

As we align with the vision, for example, of manifesting a hundred thousand pounds a month income, then there may be many beliefs such as, "No-one is able to do that, surely not someone like me, that can never happen".

It is important to note that it is very natural for negative beliefs to be triggered when we align with our hearts desires and so we must work with proficient techniques and protocols to clear these beliefs when this occurs……..

One way for us to become master manifestors is: we have to go into the deepest depths of our unconscious mind and weed out the false fear-based beliefs and the false fear-based programs that have been trapped in our sacred consciousness and locked in the vibration of fear, doubt, and limitation for aeons.

This is a fundamental aspect of shadow work, which will be shared within the sacred deck that goes along with this beautiful book.

It is very important to understand this; we are working at the level of spiritual mastery, and therefore there is no bypassing in spiritual mastery, whatsoever.

We must understand that in order for us to experience the glory of the manifestation of our holiest desires, we have to be willing to go as deep as is necessary into the depths of not only our own shadow, but our ancestral shadow, and the collective shadow, so that we can bring as much light there as is heavenly possible, that we may bring atonement and resolution to the virus program of separation, which has dominated our consciousness in this last ascension cycle.

We live in a Quantum Universe

It is so important for us all to remember that we live in a quantum universe. And every single thing that we desire, we are connected to by a string. Therefore, for us to pull through that which we wish to experience from the quantum realm, we need to build and empower that string.

When one first becomes psychically aware of the string that attaches us to all of our desires in the quantum realm, it could be understood that the string is somewhat translucent. It is then our job to empower that string and take it out of its translucent state into its solid form.

One thing that will destroy the string that attaches you to all your hearts desires in the quantum realm is doubt.

If you show up in the vibration of doubt, the string that connects you to that desire will become invisible. However, if you are lucky enough for God to present to you a sacred desire of your soul, and you, in that moment observe the string that connects you to it, and you view it with excitement and faith please know this is the most optimal way to magnetise it out of the unseen realm into the seen realm.

The way to empower the string is to embody the vibration of the desire you wish to manifest and show up in the world as she or he who has already or is already experiencing the manifestation of that desire.

Sacred Exercise

Ask yourself, how would I show up as one who has manifested my heart's desire and go on a writing rampage and explain in great detail what that looks like.

The most optimum way to do this exercise is to show up in gratitude, in deep, deep, gratitude. saying, "Thank you, God. Thank you. I had faith and I believed."

This is how you empower the string.

When you show up like this, you send Kryptonite to the string that connects you to the sacred desires of your heart.

The more that you can stand in that vibration, regardless of what is being presented to you on the third-dimensional level, the more you deeply empower that string to become solid and strong and to start appearing in your reality as direct experience.

The very definition of faith is having belief even when you cannot see it with your physical eyes. And that is, of course, a huge test on the path of spiritual mastery. As you stand in that vibration of faith, you send great, great messages and codes of information to that string, empowering that string, and then suddenly before you know it, you and that string have become one. In that moment is the moment where there is no separation, and you truly are in that vibration of gratitude because you have become one with that vibrational actualisation of your heart's desires.

When you stand in that vibration of gratitude, and anchor in that vibration of gratitude, what you will find is that what truly happens without any question of a doubt, is you will wake up the next morning and have a direct experience that the tectonic plates of your universe have shifted.

You will find that you walk in the world as someone who has completely upgraded her frequency.

You will have waiters tripping over themselves to serve you. You will receive the deepest soul smiles from your brothers and sisters when you are out and about. You will have animals and children running up to you. You will have doors opening, synchronicities occurring, alignments happening miraculously, feathers, rainbows, the works.

All of that occurs when we make those quantum shifts.

When we understand that this quantum field is essentially a game that our creator-self has given us to play with, and when we work with it in this way, and truly, truly understand what is being spoken about here, and when we embody the vibration of that which we wish to manifest and experience, this is when the shifts happen.

This is when the doors open.

This is when miracles happen.

This is when breakthroughs happen.

"Anything you can imagine is real"

—PICASSO

CHAPTER 5

MAINTAIN THE VIBRATION OF FAITH

In order to become a master manifestor, it is very, very important that you maintain the vibration of faith and stability. It is very important that you have a spiritual practice that will enable you to observe your monkey mind, and not allow your monkey mind to hinder and cloud your view through its limited perception of what is actually really occurring for you.

You are an infinite creator. You are a fractal of the creator manifested in human physical form. The moment you were born, you were encoded with the ability to call forth absolutely everything that your heart desires from the quantum realm.

In your spiritual Christ blueprint, you are truly encoded to live in that vibration of miracles, magic, and abundance. It is only virus thoughts from the matrix, from society and from your family that have blocked your innate blueprint.

It is up to you as a sovereign, powerful soul to shake off those intense lies that have been imposed upon you and the whole of humanity since time immemorial and realise that the only soul that has the right to give you permission to show up in your sovereignty is your divine self.

There is no greater spiritual authority than you

This great sacred manual that you hold in your hands, speaks of spiritual mastery at such a high level, and speaks openly about the secrets that were hidden by the mystics in all of the ancient traditions, who originally held onto the false belief that humanity was not spiritually mature enough to handle the absolute truth of who they are as innocent and profoundly powerful children of God.

Please know that in your hands, you hold a sacred and powerful scripture that has the ability to recode every lost scrambled aspect of your DNA. The truth spells in this book will enable you to reconnect with your higher self, and re-organise all previous scrambled DNA patterning's back into their perfected multidimensional 12 Strand diamond formation.........

Every single word in this transmission is absolutely connected to your soul's awakening, and is connected to activating your DNA codons, and the light that you hold in your DNA that is infused with your true Self/God codes.

Please know that when one speaks about the Self codes, we are always speaking about the Christ Self codes because the Self is with a capital S and the Self is God.

The Self and God are one. There is no separation from God and the Self. The Self and God are one.

We are all fractals of the one God Self, and because of that we inevitably have access to the infinite quantum realms, and it is through the power and the discipline of our own consciousness that we activate, access, and pull through the truth and energy from those quantum realms - from the realm of the unseen into the realm of the seen and the known.

When we truly commit to standing in the embodiment and the vibrational reality of our prayer already being answered, then a miracle happens and we vibrationally pop out of one holographic reality into an upgraded holographic reality which reflects our new embodied frequency.

This is how the universe works. If you go to God with a begging bowl praying, the universe says, "Oh wow, look at that God being! She's showing up begging. It looks like she's locked into the vibration of lack and she's praying for more lack. We better give her more lack."

However, if you show up to God saying, "My cup is so overfull, my cup is overflowing God, I'm so grateful. How can I serve you God? How can I serve my brothers and sisters? How can I bring more light and joy into this world, where the people are so spiritually starved, and the mind control has run so deep?"

When I show up in that way, miracles invariably happen, timelines shift, old timelines collapse, and we activate the quantum field.

The trick is to become the vibration of that which you want to experience to the point that there is absolutely zero lack consciousness left in your psychic field.

This means that you have reached a point where you are absolutely genuinely experiencing it, to the point that you actually don't need it anymore.

This is the true phenomenon that occurs when we work at this level of embodiment. And that is almost the precise moment when that which you are aligning with has zero resistance in the quantum field and thus will come knocking on your door.

Please understand that this transmission is being bought through at an extremely powerful and auspicious time with my own evolutionary process.

And it is truly encoded with the highest spiritual Gnosis that my soul has ever brought through, particularly in the realms of working with the quantum field in order to absolutely embody being a master manifestor.

The path to becoming a master manifestor is to understand that you are a master.

And a very good question to start with is:

How does a master move about in the world?

The answer is: A master is at one with the zero-point field, and

A master realises that the present moment is the zero-point field.

A master remembers that time doesn't exist, that she is a quantum time traveller, and through the direction of her own consciousness (which is no longer hijacked by the matrix) she is able to quantum travel to any dimensional reality, to any timeline, to any desire she wishes to experience as an awakened Avatar master soul.

When you show up in the world at this level of awakening, this is when we show up truly as the spiritual master that we have incarnated to be.

We ignite a raging fire that burns within our soul that can be witnessed by all of our brothers and sisters in a way that is purely the vibration of home, warmth, beauty, kindness, and deep, deep, sacred wisdom.

You owe it to your brothers and sisters to awaken in this lifetime.

You owe it to your brothers and sisters to own your spiritual mastery. You promised your brothers and sisters that you would be the one to hold the mantle of leadership on the spiritual level for your divine masculine Twin Flame if you are a divine feminine polarity Twin Flame.

As you awaken to your divinity, as you take ownership of your innocence, as you stand in your power and embodiment and rebel against the matrix in all its distorted patterning's, you become an illuminated master within this third-dimensional frequency band. This serves to create a powerful magnetic field of light for all your brothers and sisters who will be magnetised to you, when they need a stabilised light force.

In order to become a master manifestor, we must remember that we are worthy and deserving of all the riches of the Kingdom of God.

The 3D matrix has sought to implement a false notion of sin, guilt and shame onto the innocent children of the Divine, and this has created a huge filter or block you could say, that has prevented our pure and pristine manifestational powers to be actualised directly by us.

This is an affliction that has been cast upon every child on earth unless you were born to completely enlightened parents.

CHAPTER 6

NERVOUS SYSTEM RECALIBRATION

In this chapter, I would like to speak about a very important aspect of manifestation, and that is the nervous system and the extent to which the nervous system is calibrated to a feeling and vibrational experience of safety and belonging.

For many of us that have incarnated into the third-dimensional prism matrix, we have experienced all sorts of programming and indoctrination that has ensured that our belief system is not calibrated to the God source-code within us.

Many of us have been deeply programmed by all aspects of society, from our families to the media, to politicians, to the education system, and religion, to believe that we are individualised, separate drops of water with no sense of belonging or orientation in the world.

This false notion has served the old controllers, as it has ensured that humanity is out of alignment with their true spiritual power.

All of this programming has had a huge detrimental effect on the collective nervous system of humanity.

On top of this, many people in our society have been heinously abused by their parents. Many have experienced sexual abuse, physical abuse, emotional abuse, and psychological abuse.

When a child experiences abuse, this can very often activate a splitting of the psyche.

The reason for this is the part of the psyche that experiences the trauma is unable to understand or process the abuse, which activates a split in the psyche.

When one is operating from a split psyche, they are operating with minimal energetic efficiency, as precious sacred energy will be siphoned off towards the separate and lost aspect of the self.

The splitting of the psyche has a huge detrimental effect on the nervous system, as this ensures one does not feel safe and comfortable and at home in one's physical body.

When we do not feel at home in our physical body, this means that we are not anchored and we are not plugged into the present moment. And are therefore much more likely and vulnerable to be influenced by nefarious agendas that are perpetually seeking to keep our attention anchored away from the present moment.

When we have experienced deep trauma, it is very difficult for us to plug into the God source-code within us. The God source-code within us is our true divine blueprint that will remain eternally with us throughout all our incarnational cycles. This is also deeply connected to our higher-self template.

It is very important, this conjecture, to remember deeply that no one is a victim.

Everything that we experience in our lifetime is designed by us and our higher self and our divine counterpart whilst sat at the feet of Mother-Father-God.

We choose the lessons that we need to learn in this lifetime. We choose the characters that are going to love us, and we choose the characters that are going to hurt us and betray us. We are never ever a victim. Everything that is created in our life has been set up by us to bring us to our enlightenment, often through the law of polarity and duality.

It is very important that everyone reading these words address the elephant in the room, which is the unstabilised nervous system. If you really want to become a master manifester, you have to realize that you are home within your own divine self.

You have to realize that you are the one that your soul has been seeking, and that the God source-code within you has been placed in the safest place of all, and that is within your deepest being.

Mother-Father-God would never, ever place your source of alignment, happiness and security outside of you, as Mother-Father-God is a good and great God and would never create a situation where you could be eternally cut off from source energy.

Therefore, it is up to you to understand and bring yourself home to the present moment, in order to stabilise your own nervous system, that you may understand that you hold the God source-code within you, and through your own choices and achievements, you can attune to this God source-code within you.

When you do that, you will experience the profound stabilisation of your nervous system.

The nervous system is the foundation of our consciousness. If we do not have a stabilised nervous system, it is absolutely impossible for us to build our spiritual destiny and our spiritual dreams. Once we calibrate our nervous system back to the God source-code within, this is the solid foundation that our soul needs in order to build, align and manifest with our deepest spiritual destiny.

There is much to speak about the nervous system, and I do hope that this chapter has brought you a deeper understanding and clarity surrounding the importance of having a stabilised and calibrated nervous system when it comes to manifesting our heart's greatest spiritual destiny.

"If you wish to find the secrets of the universe think of energy, frequency and vibration."

—NIKOLA TESLA

CHAPTER 7

THE IMPORTANCE OF BOUNDARIES ON THE PATH OF MANIFESTATION MASTERY

When we embark on the path of becoming a master manifestor, it is absolutely imperative that we understand that we have to clear all false programming that prevents us from standing in our true values and our true self-worth.

One who is showing up in the world, standing in her true self-worth has extremely vigilant boundaries and will not allow anyone into her sacred space who does not come with the energy of recognition of her as a child of the Divine and who does not come with honour, respect, and abiding love.

When we attain this level of self-love and spiritual mastery, we collapse all timelines pertaining to the false matrix indoctrination, which has entrained everyone to believe that we are unworthy to receive the profound riches of the Kingdom of our Mother-Father God in Heaven.

Therefore, for you to become a master manifestor, it is absolutely imperative that you identify all of the beliefs and programs in your consciousness that have you fixated on the false, low timeline of feeling unworthy of your heart's desires.

Some of the thoughts which you may identify with are:

- Nothing good ever happens to me.
- Everyone else is worthy. I am not worthy.
- Why does nothing good ever happen to me?
- I am so unlucky.
- I do not deserve to be rich.
- Money and abundance are hard to come by.
- You always have to work very hard for abundance and to be rich.

These are examples of the beliefs that many of us are holding, and which deeply and profoundly block our manifestational powers.

Sacred Exercise

Please take out a piece of paper and write a list of all of the programs, all of the thoughts and beliefs that you have around financial abundance. Please write out all of your programming around financial abundance and your parents' beliefs, starting with your mother then your father and include your grandparents too - write out phrases you heard often i.e. "Money doesn't grow on trees." etc.

Please identify the programs that have been consciously and unconsciously instilled within you. Please write out all of these programs and any programs that you have collected from society at large.

In order to get the most out of this exercise, please take out your journal now and write out all of your heart's desires. Write out your wildest dreams with regards to your life - Please do not hold back!

Next write out all of the false beliefs and programs that you have about manifesting those specific desires.

Please go through all of your hearts desires individually sharing all of your limited beliefs.

When you have completed both of these exercises - please thank your limited beliefs and old programming, and then call upon St Germain and the Violet Flame.

Visualise handing this paper to Saint-Germain for him to transmute in the Violet Flame - as this is occurring you can take out a flame and burn those pieces of paper...

CHAPTER 8

THE FEMININE ASPECT OF MANIFESTATION

In order to become a master manifestor, we have to work with our masculine and feminine energy. As we step into becoming master manifestors, it is very important that we work with the magnetic aspect of our consciousness. We need to work with a balance of both these energies in order to quickly align vibrationally with our hearts desires.

Our feminine energy is intricately connected to receivership and mastery of this polarity principle and how adept we are at receiving the blessings that our higher self has stored for us in this lifetime.

Part of the patriarchal programming has suppressed the importance and brilliance of this particular ascension codon, but if you are reading these words, I highly recommend that you work on empowering the left feminine side of your body and prime her to receive all the great blessings that are lined up for her in her spiritual destiny.

Sacred Exercise

To do this, focus on empowering your receivership codes by sending light to the left side of your body and visualising the left side of your body, particularly your left palm receiving light codes that are calibrated towards re-coding you to be able to receive blessings from an extremely high vibration, that is your higher self.

There are other aspects to the feminine part of manifestation, which I will speak about later on in this manual. But I would like to say that it is very important that we don't just sit on our rear ends visualising that which we wish to manifest.

In order to align with our hearts desires, we have to take actions every day that are moving us towards this alignment and manifestation.

An extremely top ascension tip is to do something today that your future self will thank you for.

This is very, very powerful guidance, which encourages us to work with our masculine energy in order to stay in action around our manifestations.

CHAPTER 9

THE MASCULINE ASPECTS OF MANIFESTATION

It is important to know that if you do not take action towards your hearts desires, then the universe cannot rise to meet you on your quest to manifest your hearts desires, as it is only when we take action and go to the place or send the letter or reach out to the person that we have been guided to reach out to that the universe then can rise and meet us at that level of action.

If you do not take any action and stay stuck simply visualising, then it is very, very difficult for the universe to rise and meet you and support you to manifest your hearts intentions. Therefore, the importance of taking action cannot be stressed enough when we are seeking to become a master manifestor.

The most important aspect that we need to remember on our journey to becoming a master manifestor is that we live in a vibrational universe. And I know that I have said this before, but I will keep on repeating it because we've all been so detrimentally programmed, that we actually need to experience repetitive statements in order to counterbalance the nefarious indoctrination we've all been subjected to.

So, for you to become a master manifestor, it is absolutely imperative that you remember that we live in a vibrational universe and that your heart's desires already exist on a particular timeline or in a particular vibrational reality.

Therefore, in order for you to experience the manifestation of your heart's desires, you have to become the vibration of that which you are praying for.

This is the only way, and this is the fast track for you to draw into your holographic reality, that which has been encoded into your heart via wishes and desires.

How do I embody the vibration of that which I wish to manifest?

You may be asking how do I embody the vibration of that which I wish to manifest? And that is a very great and valid question.

You embody the vibration by choosing to and attuning to the vibration of the fulfilment of your hearts desires.

For example, if you wish to manifest a particular relationship with your divine counterpart, you have to wake up in the morning as she who has already manifested that reality and is experiencing that. And you must go about your day as though you are already having that experience.

When you show up in the world as she who has already manifested her hearts desires you move in a different way, your body language is different, your tone is sweeter, your tips are bigger, your smile is brighter, and your kindness is palpable. Remember to keep showing up as the version that you are moving towards in order to fast track your manifestation timeline.

"For verily I say unto you, If ye have faith as a grain of mustard seed, ye shall say unto this mountain, Remove hence to yonder place, and it shall remove, and nothing shall be impossible unto you."

—MATTHEW 17:20

CHAPTER 10

QUANTUM MANIFESTATION

It is important for us all to remember that we coexist in a quantum realm. Quantum refers to multi-dimensional timelines operating concurrently within the zero-point field, the present moment of now.

Quantum refers to nonlinear.

Quantum refers to laws beyond the restrictions of the third-dimensional matrix.

What we have to understand is that all of our sacred and beautiful hearts desires are encoded in our heart consciousness by God, our creator, and we stay connected to these desires via a string.

There are many ways for us to empower the string that connects us to our hearts desires, and I would like to now share a few of those ways.

We empower the string of our hearts desires and turn it from a translucent state to a much more fixed and solid state by believing in the accuracy of our dreams, believing that they are not random, and holding a deep knowing that they are specifically chosen by our higher-self prior to our incarnation, and are deeply and intricately connected to the fulfilment of our spiritual destiny in this lifetime.

We empower the string connecting us to our desires in the quantum realm by speaking as though that which we wish to manifest has already manifest. When we speak, we are casting spells, and sacred scriptures state, "In the beginning was the word" and that is because the word is all powerful.

In order to empower our strings in the quantum realm, we speak as though our desires have already manifested right now.

I am reminded of a wonderful anecdote. I heard recently about a village in South America, where there was a very long drought. All of the villagers were asked to please come together to pray for the rain, so on the day this was planned, all of the villagers turned up and got on their knees and begged God to send them rain, but there was only one little boy that turned up with an umbrella.

As soon as he arrived, he put up his umbrella, and stood in absolute faith that God was going to send the rain. And of course, the heavens opened, and the rain came.

This is one of the most powerful manifestation anecdotes that you could possibly be exposed to. You have to show up in life in this so-called reality, as the vibration of one who has manifested that which you are calling forth from the unseen realms.

You have to show up in 100% faith that that which you are aligning with has manifested and is manifesting.

Another way to empower the string that connects us to our hearts desires in the quantum realm is to work on having conversations with yourself, to convince yourself to expand to a level to be able to hold that which you are wishing to manifest.

For example, if you are wishing to manifest a £100,000 income per month, then it is highly advisable that you have a conversation with yourself, convincing yourself of the validity and efficacy of this.

If that was me, I would be using terms such as:

"It was so easy to reach my first £100,000 a month. I applied all of the principles of sacred manifestation and I aligned with it instantly. I now consistently earn £100,000 a month."

When we put forward these statements and affirmations, either in our own consciousness or written down on paper, this deeply and profoundly empowers the timeline whereby we experience the reality of our hearts deepest prayers being answered.

CHAPTER 11

LAW OF POLARITY

There is one aspect of manifestation that I would like to speak about now, and that is the law of polarity and how it relates to manifestation. This is an extremely important and deep subject matter, and I will do my best to share with you what I have learned, remembered, and understood about this particular law.

Every soul that is incarnated alive has chosen to incarnate into a third-dimensional prison matrix.

As the soul incarnates into the third-dimensional limitation matrix, a bombardment of programmings and limiting beliefs are entrained and somewhat forced into the innocent soul's consciousness field via the programming of society - through the family, through the school system, through the media, through religion, and indeed, all aspects of society which are very much orientated towards the third-dimensional limitation paradigm.

Therefore, when we embark on the path of spiritual mastery and engage with the notion of becoming a master manifestor, we remember that our desires are extremely holy and extremely sacred, and indeed, we are extremely blessed to bear witness to one of our holy sacred desires of our heart.

In that moment where the desire is revealed to us, for example, the desire to manifest a relationship on the physical plane with your Twin Flame or ascension partner or God mate, when you become aware of that desire to unite with your Twin Flame or manifest £1,000,000, you will notice that many limiting beliefs will spring up connected to that desire such as:

- I'm so unlucky in love.
- That will never happen for me.
- No one in my family has had a happy relationship.
- I don't know what a happy relationship looks like.
- That's just not my destiny.

These thoughts will come from the egoic consciousness, which is another way of saying the wounded aspect of the Self, the part of the consciousness that has received somewhat of a battering whilst being incarnated into this third-dimensional matrix.

Therefore, in order for us to manifest our hearts desire, it is absolutely necessary for us to face our limiting beliefs. This can be viewed as shadow work, the facing and embracing the hidden thoughts that are inherently and innately sabotaging your ability to align vibrationally with your heart's desire.

This relates to the law of polarity because we have to be courageous and willing enough to look at our darkness and look at our shadow belief structures in order to bring light to them and atonement to them, so that ultimately, we can decide that they are no longer serving us and indeed it is appropriate for us to let them go.

In order to attain the highest heights of the manifestation of our desires, we must be able to go into the deeper work of examining our limiting beliefs which are blocking us from aligning vibrationally with our sacred hearts desires.

When we do this deep, profound shadow work, we transform old archaic timelines, and we also rewrite the neural pathways in our brain.

There are many techniques that we can use to face our darkness and face our shadow beliefs. A technique that I would highly recommend working with is asking yourself the question, What part of me gets to be validated by holding on to this limiting belief? or What part of me gets to be seen by me holding onto these limited beliefs?

This is an extremely powerful and game-changing question to be asking ourselves on our path of spiritual and manifestation mastery.

You will find that if you explore your limiting beliefs, there is very often an egoic addiction to remaining in victim mode, to proving that God has abandoned you, to holding on to limiting beliefs that you are innately unlucky and unworthy.

So very often, the limiting beliefs that are specifically blocking our manifestations are validating our beliefs about life and are creating proof that, indeed, this is a challenging realm, and we are being perpetually abandoned by our Creator.

While there are many techniques that we can use to bring light to our shadow side, the most important thing we need to understand is that our ability to face our darkness, our shadow and our limiting beliefs automatically creates the polarity experience of enabling us to experience the highest heights of the manifestation of our desires.

I am reminded of a Kahlil Gibran saying:

> *"The deeper that sorrow*
> *carves into your being,*
> *the more joy*
> *you can contain."*

Gibran reminds us that our sorrow is much like ground that is being dug out, but the ground is being dug out in order to hold the depth of our joy. The amount of joy we can hold depends on how much sorrow we have dug up.

We experience sorrow in the absence of our joy, which confirms that everything that we desire, we truly are programmed and coded to manifest.

And so, if we experience sorrow by not experiencing something on the physical level, the reason why we are experiencing that sorrow is because the thing that we are aligning with is deeply programmed to bring us profound joy, and the absence of that is causing us sorrow.

All of the greatest teachers who teach about the law of attraction, the law of manifestation and the law of vibration share deeply and prolifically about the law of polarity and how this relates to manifestation.

One has to be able to face their deepest, darkest shadow beliefs in order to bring the light to these places. And clear all unconscious beliefs and blocks that are preventing the alignment and manifestation of our sacred heart desires.

"You are never too old to set another goal, or to dream a new dream"

—C S LEWIS

CHAPTER 12

MORE ON THE POLARITY OF MANIFESTATION

I would like to now devote the next chapter to speaking about something that is a very important aspect of the manifestation process, and that is: how the shadow aspect is intricately connected to our capacity to be a successful master manifestor.

Whenever we expose ourselves to great light, be that in a person or a frequency, this can invariably expose our shadow unconscious aspects.

Our shadow aspects refer to the part of us that perceive themselves as cut off from source energy and are trapped in a paradigm of aloneness and separation.

When we encounter light in its purest form, it has the ability to expose all hidden aspects in order for them to be exposed and ultimately brought home to the light.

This is deeply connected to the manifestation process.

Sometimes when we are blocked in manifesting a specific thing, it is because there is a part of us that wishes to be validated by us not experiencing that which our heart desires to manifest.

So, on your journey of manifestation, I would highly recommend that you spend time in self-enquiry and enquire into what part of you gets to be deeply endorsed if you do not experience your hearts manifestation.

Many of us have experienced profound wounding in our life. And this wounding can often get triggered when we expand our consciousness and grow into our higher dimensional mastery.

It is always important to remember that our triggers are our greatest gifts on the spiritual path as they shine an important light on that which was previously hidden from us, and there is nothing like a trigger to catapult us to the next level, to assist us to stabilise in fifth-dimensional consciousness.

Please let me give you an example;

Say I wanted to heal my relationship with my friends, and I've been working on manifesting that, but it hasn't come to fruition yet.

If that is the case, I would set myself on a trajectory of enquiry.

I would enquire about what part of myself gets to be right, and what part of myself gets to be sanctioned by me having this experience of not experiencing the fulfilment of the manifestation of my hearts desires?

The answer could be, I get to be right about being abandoned by God.

I get to be right about the fact that I'm always unlucky.

I get to prove that my egoic perception of reality is true.

This situation endorses my belief about myself, that no one loves me….

And I'm actually more invested in believing that thought, than having a breakthrough with that belief.

Sacred Exercise

Please take out your journal and write out an unfiltered stream of consciousness, around what part of you gets to be right if you do not experience the manifestation of your heart's desires, remembering that this is invariably connected to the ego and the validation the ego gets by not having the experience of manifesting your hearts desires.

This is an extremely powerful and potent way to clear resistance and clear all the weeds that are preventing the beautiful seed and flower of your hearts desires to grow in the garden of your consciousness.

These weeds, these thoughts, these beliefs hold great, great power over our subconscious mind and have the ability to absolutely and entirely block the manifestation process, but they can only do that if they are operating in the darkness in the shadows.

The moment we turn to face those old thoughts and beliefs, this immediately starts affecting the vibratory patterning of the belief and it starts collapsing in and of itself.

May I take this opportunity to remind you that a program is only a program if it is unconscious. The moment a program becomes conscious, it becomes a choice. So, all of these opportunities are gifts and invitations for us to integrate deeper levels of the shadow aspect within us that simply has not awoken to the light of God source energy within...

*"Logic will take you from A to B.
Imagination will take you everywhere."*

—EINSTEIN

CHAPTER 13

MANIFESTATION AND THE ART OF SURRENDER

I would like to devote the next part of this sacred manuscript to speaking about this, bearing in mind that every single thing that our heart desires is connected to us via a string in the quantum field.

It is so important for us to all remember that there is a doorway that exists within the quantum field, and behind the doorway exists our heart's desire. We have a string that eternally connects us to our hearts desire, and the way we open that doorway is through becoming an energetic match to the frequency that exists beyond that doorway.

There are many tools and techniques that we have spoken about in great depth that enable us to attune to or indeed choose to align with the frequency of our heart's desires. But what about the extremely important and potent subject matter of surrender? What about letting go? and how does this relate to the important matter of manifestation mastery?

My experience of this is, it could be likened to sitting on my patio, drinking the finest Kombucha, or in the olden days, it would have been Champagne celebrating the fact that I got the call from God that the very thing that I ordered is being delivered to me. And I would approach it in the way of absolute celebration, living in the knowing, the deep, deep knowing that, that which I have aligned with on a frequency level is indeed making its way to me as we speak.

This means that I don't have to think about it. I don't have to be constantly checking the door, checking the post, ringing up Royal Mail to see where my delivery is. I can just simply get on with my day and get on with co-creating all the other spectacular, joyful, and miraculous things I wish to experience in my reality.

Letting go is letting go of our attachment to how that which we have aligned with on a frequency level will come into our physical world. It is deeply about letting go of the mind's incessant need to understand the logic that sits behind the how's of manifesting our hearts desires, working with the quantum field.

Whenever we engage in this dialogue or narrative within our own consciousness, we immediately drop out a fifth-dimensional consciousness and we go into a 4D and 3D state, as questioning the how's is very much of the intellectual realm, a realm that exists outside of the zero-point field and multi-dimensionality, indeed the realm of illusion. The dualistic realm of the third-dimensional matrix.

Therefore, it is never appropriate for us to wonder about the how's with which our sacred hearts desires will manifest for us in our lives. It is our job to hold the frequency and hold the knowing that they are indeed on their way, and God is delivering them right now. The delivery driver is driving through the streets near your hometown, on his way to deliver you your package.

You can apply this concept to any area of manifestation. Knowing that, that which you wish to manifest is on its way. There's nothing to stress about, as it's an absolute 100% fact. It's on its way. When we can stand in this much trust, it's very easy for us to let go and get on with other aspects of our lives, other aspects of our day, other creative endeavours. We let go of the incessant need to wait and watch and forever check in to see if there's any change. This could be likened to watching paint dry or watching a plant grow.

I am reminded of the saying "A watched kettle never boils." This saying has brought me so much truth throughout my journey so far, and points directly to the message of this entire chapter, which is about reminding us of the potency we can activate when we let go.

When we let go, we trust implicitly that, that which we wish to manifest is on its way to us.

You have done the work, and you can keep doing the work. You can keep attuning to the frequency in a joyful and playful way, but you never ever have to worry about the how's or the when's or the whys or the who withs or the what ifs. That's not your job. Your job is to hold the creative vision, the creative knowing, the deep conviction, faith, and internal belief that that which you desire is already yours.

In those words, there lies the entire decoded mystery of this sacred manuscript.

All that you desire is already yours.

May you take these words and breathe them deep into yourselves, and may they nourish your cells with the replenishment that they are so in need of in this forgetful matrix that we, ourselves have all been so brave to incarnate into.

It is my deepest honour to bring through this sacred manual, and I pray that you meditate on these powerful words, that your desires are already yours, knowing that when you truly allow yourself to drop your fearful ego narrative, which continuously keeps you in separation from this truth, you clear all deep intrinsic resistance to the physicalisation and actualisation of your sacred heart desires.

The time is now, sovereign ones, for you to take up your mantle, to take your crown out of the etheric realm and place it firmly on your head. Stand tall and stand proud as an awakened and luminous child of God. One who stands tall in remembrance of her divine and eternal innocence as an offspring of the most high.

Remember your promise to your brothers and sisters that you would wear your crown with pride. Remember the promise that you made to so many souls who were so afraid to incarnate back into this dualistic matrix. You promised them that you would remember, and through your light, they would recognise their own Divine and eternal light.

So may you take the words from this sacred manual deep into your heart, and may you allow the codes of spiritual mastery to activate within your 144 codon DNA patterning.

We are all children of God. We are all children of the Divine. We are all fractals of the one diamond source that has many names and which many, including myself, call God.

"When you want something the whole universe will conspire for you to have it"

—PAULO COHELLO

CHAPTER 14

TRANSFORM YOUR THOUGHTS AND DESIRES FROM 3D TO 5D

I would like to now devote the next chapter to speaking about manifestation mastery and how we transform our thoughts and desires in the third-dimension to the desired outcome in the fifth-dimension.

I was speaking to an incredible friend and mentor of mine a few days ago, and she shared with me the most amazing analogy which I would love to share with you. She reminded me that manifestation could be likened to a kettle of boiling water. The kettle of boiling water represents our third-dimensional reality whereby we begin to apply manifestation principles such as consistency, visualisation, acting as if, and scripting for example.

When we apply these tools to our third-dimensional reality, this activates a shift and a transformation activating the water in the kettle to become steam. This could be likened to the fourth-dimensional aspect of the manifestation process.

If we keep up the momentum and the consistency and keep visualising and acting as if that which we wish to manifest has already happened, then we can observe that the steam will transform and become a singular droplet of water.

As the water drops from the steam, this represents the fifth-dimensional desired manifestation.

This an extremely powerful and potent analogy that explains deeply the fundamental principles of manifestation.

This guides us to the living truth that we are all extremely powerful manifesters, and all we need to do to manifest anything from the unseen realm is simply apply a few spiritual tools to be able to transform the water in the kettle into steam, which then become the fifth-dimensional droplets that form from the steam.

As soon as we truly understand and grasp this analogy, the question becomes how do we maintain the momentum of keeping the water boiling in the kettle? Because clearly, it is the boiling water in the kettle which transforms the water to steam, which then transforms it to become a droplet of water. So truly the question is, how do we maintain the momentum of the boiling water in the kettle?

I would like to now divulge a few of those ways that I have discovered to keep the kettle boiling.

1. Belief in yourself, belief that we live in a magical universe and our desires are holy, and If we are privileged enough to recognise the holy desire of our heart, we absolutely have been gifted with the tools to be able to manifest them from the unseen realm to the seen realm. Knowing this at the deepest level is the first fundamental principle of manifestation.

2. We need to understand that what we desire is already available to us in the quantum field, that we live in a frequency universe and the only way for us to experience the whole dimensional aspect of something in the quantum field is for us to become a vibrational match to it.

For example, if we wish to manifest devotion and love from a Twin Flame, we must apply that devotion and love to ourselves and to all of our relationships. We literally must match the frequency of that which we wish to manifest.

3. Consistency is a fundamental aspect of manifestation mastery. It is a waste of time to apply heat to the water and then allow the water to become cool again and then the next day, add heat again. It is much more powerful to maintain a vibration of consistency. This refers to applying a regular manifestation practice into your daily spiritual maintenance.

4. Scripting, which as I've already mentioned is writing out your manifestation as though it has already manifested and is one of the most powerful and potent ways to draw your manifestations from the unseen realm into the seen realm.

5. Your faith and belief is what will move mountains and transform your overall experience of third-dimensional reality into fifth-dimensional reality.

CHAPTER 15

CONSISTENCY IS KEY

As discussed in the previous chapter I shared with you the analogy of the boiling water and the precipitation process that is activated when we boil water, and it became steam and then forms droplets of distilled water. I spoke about how we can apply these principles to our manifestation protocols, but I will say that in order to experience the precipitation protocol we absolutely do need to apply consistency. I spoke about consistency briefly in the previous chapter but I would like to spend a few moments speaking about it in further depth......

What does a consistent manifestation protocol practice look like?

- For me, having a committed manifestation protocol practice means that I commit to my current protocol at least three or four times every day.
- It means maintaining a vibration of consistency with that which I wish to manifest, and not jumping from one thing to the other.
- Manifestation requires focus, which is also connected to the vibration of faith.
- We cannot manifest anything out of the unseen realm if we do not have faith.
- It's very important that we maintain a high level of faith if we want to experience the manifestation of our heart's desires from 3D to 5D.

There are many, many other aspects of manifestation mastery which have been covered in this book. But it is very important that everyone understands we must transform our base third-dimensional thought forms into direct emotional experiences in order to inform our subconscious mind that we are having this as a direct experience.

For example, if I say to you now, imagine sucking a lemon, and you imagined it, your mouth will start watering and that is because your subconscious mind does not know the difference between something that is imagined and something that is real.

It is very, very important that we apply this principle to all aspects of manifestation by truly, absolutely, deeply engaging our subconscious mind through all of our senses, sight, sound, smell, taste, touch to fully experience the fulfilment of our manifestation on an imaginal level.

"You can do anything you want to do,
Let your mind body and soul do it,
Prove it to yourself and say I want,
I will,
I can do anything,
I know I can fulfill my dreams"

—INJOY

CHAPTER 16

GRATITUDE

I would like to now take this opportunity to speak about the extremely important subject matter of gratitude.

If you are seriously committing to the path of becoming a master manifestor, there are no words that can adequately express how important it is for you to integrate a practice of gratitude into your day-to-day reality. Whenever we focus on gratitude, we are orientating our consciousness away from lack towards that, which we wish to manifest.

This is an act of spiritual mastery to direct our consciousness anywhere other than where our egoic consciousness is blindly leading us. The simple act of deciding to go on a rampage of gratitude is in and of itself extremely powerful and life-changing, and you will experience the most phenomenal results in record speed when you commit to this path.

Whenever we apply the energy and the vibration of gratitude to any area of our life, we are literally opening the floodgates to experience more. This is because light attracts light, and so if we fill up our consciousness with thoughts of gratitude, then we are simply informing our subconscious mind to send us more things to be grateful for.

You can apply this to any area of your life, particularly an area that you are struggling with. For example, if you are struggling in your relationship at the moment and feel very confident that you are meant to be with your partner, instead of obsessively focusing on all of the things that you are annoyed and irritated about in your relationship, decide every day to focus on the aspects of your relationship that you deeply love and appreciate. Go on rampages of gratitude about your partner, about all the things that you love about him or her. And remember back to the time when you first got together and all the things that you really loved and were attracted to in your partner.

This one technique has saved so many relationships, and you can apply this to any area of your life. Say, for example, you are experiencing a lack in your finances. You can go on a rampage of gratitude giving thanks for all the money that you have had, all the things that you have bought, all the things that money can't buy, all the amazing things that you are able to buy. It is very important that you focus on the things that you can manifest such as a roof over your head, food on your table, friendships that activate belly laughs within you. There is so much that you can be grateful for, and when you deeply commit to the path of gratitude, you will experience a fundamental and profound shift in your reality.

I learned about the power of gratitude in 2011 and quickly realised that I was using a huge amount of my energy on focusing on that, which I didn't wish to manifest. I decided then and there that I would never ever do that again, and that I would absolutely completely commit to the path of gratitude. Since doing that, I have experienced extraordinary levels of happiness and peace in my everyday reality, and I've experienced all of my dreams coming true. We really must take ownership and guardianship of our consciousness because if we don't then the deep state, the cabal, the matrix will.

My two fundamental reasons for why I advocate committing to the path of gratitude are that first of all, every time we choose to go on a rampage of gratitude, we take ownership and direction of our consciousness, and we direct it towards that, which we wish to think about, and experience as opposed to it being dragged along by our egoic consciousness, which doesn't know its backside from its elbow.

And the other reason is that it truly transforms our spiritual baseline vibration. We experience greater alignment, greater happiness, greater levels of wealth, greater levels of manifestation and the experience of all of our dreams coming true.

Sacred Exercise

There are so many aspects to the path of gratitude, which I haven't covered, and I would love you to take a moment to think about all the ways that gratitude has hugely enhanced and affected your life. please take out a pen and paper now and go on a rampage of gratitude.....

The path of gratitude is the path of spiritual mastery. The spiritual master understands that there is a battle going on for our consciousness and unless we direct our consciousness to that which we wish to manifest, the matrix will pull us into thoughts that are co-creating the dystopian world that the matrix wishes to impose upon us. I hope and pray that you gain clarity from this chapter and that you truly commit to the path of gratitude as a fundamental alignment with your spiritual mastery codes.

CHAPTER 17

EMPTINESS AND MANIFESTATION

It is very important that everyone who is reading these words understands the importance of emptiness on the spiritual path.

Every instrument is empty. A guitar is hollow. A drum is hollow. A flute is hollow. Why is that?

Every instrument is empty so that they may receive the grace of God, the grace of the Christed spirit.

If we are deeply committed to becoming master manifestors, it is up to all of us individually to find spiritual practices that bring us to the vibration of emptiness, because if we are filled up with our victim story and victim narrative, "he did that, and she said that, and he said that etc," then we are experiencing the very opposite of emptiness.

When we are in victim mode, we are very much cut off from receiving the divine grace of the Christed spirit, the holy spirit, that is all around us.

So, if you are vibrationally drawn to these words, I would assume that you are on the path of spiritual mastery. And therefore, I would like to remind you of the importance of committing to a path of emptiness.

Finding a spiritual practice to bring you to emptiness is a powerful way to align yourself with the zero-point field.

My spiritual practice is resting as awareness for short moments. I have been committed to this spiritual practice since 2012, when I met the amazing group called Balanced View. They had readapted a 6,000-year-old Buddhist practice for the modern mind and the modern audience.

When I was privileged enough to encounter this phenomenal spiritual practice, it didn't take me long to decide that I would deeply commit to the practice of resting as awareness for short moments, and I would be committed to stopping thinking whenever I naturally remembered to do so.

This spiritual practice brought me to the zero-point field very, very quickly and very, very rapidly. And I have been able to stabilise at the zero-point field since 2013.

There are many spiritual practises that will bring you to the zero-point field. For some, it is acting. For some, it is painting. For some, it is walking. For some, it is movement. For some, it is meditating. For some, it is mindfulness.

There are infinite ways to bring you to emptiness, but the most important message is for you to find a practice and commit to it.

Spiritual mastery is not for the fainthearted. Everyone who places themselves on this path must understand that it is the path for the spiritual olympian.

You will not get anywhere on the spiritual enlightenment path if you practice the protocol for a week or two. Everything that I have shared in this book deserves to be adopted as a lifelong spiritual practice.

All of the manifestation protocols, all of the meditation protocols, all of the emptiness protocols, none of it will work unless you commit avidly and deeply to a lifelong practice.

To dip one toe in for a week will get you absolutely nowhere. And I would even suggest that you are wasting your time and to not even bother. In a situation such as this it would be my recommendation that you come back to this material when you are ready to jump in with two feet and commit deeply and profoundly to this work.

We have covered so much in this book. And one of the things that I would most like to leave you with is the remembrance of the exquisite nature of your heart's desires and the fact that your hearts desires are curated by your higher self in accordance with the tapestry of the higher self of every member of the human family.

Therefore, if you deny the validity of your hearts desires, you are activating a deficit within the tapestry of creation. And this will have a knock-on effect on many, many, many souls.

May everyone reading these words understand and own their true spiritual power. And hold the remembrance that if you have a sacred desire in your heart, you have every tool imaginable within you to be able to manifest that.

There is absolutely nothing that you cannot manifest if you hold that desire in your heart.

It is very important now that we evolve spiritually as a human family and we take our place as emotionally mature and spiritually mature humans, understanding that we are co-creating our holographic reality based upon our beliefs and programs.

Please remember that a program is only a program if it's unconscious. The moment a program becomes conscious, it then becomes a choice. So therefore, we are duty bound to identify all of our limited programming and make choices that are in alignment with our true, godly spiritual nature.

It is my deepest pleasure to serve you all, my brothers and sisters. And please enjoy working with the exquisite Oracle deck that accompanies this powerful, life changing book.

"The eternal law of life is: What you think and feel you bring Into form, Where your thoughts are you are, for you are your Consciousness, and what you meditate upon you create"

—ST GERMAIN

CHAPTER 18

EMOTIONS AND MANIFESTATION

In the following chapter, I would like to share a very, very powerful and potent manifestation hack.

So many teachers who speak about manifestation and the law of attraction and the law of frequency will speak in depth about how the quantum field is deeply connected to our emotions and will often share that what we experience on the emotional level turbo boosts, the manifestation of our heart's desires on the quantum level.

Very often, when we have visualisation practises, it is quite challenging to access the deep emotions on demand, as often our deep emotional experiences happen spontaneously and not as and when we lie down on the yoga mat to experience them.

What I have found is that one of the potent ways you can manifest proficiently and with great ease is if you apply the principles of manifestation mastery to times in your life where you experience an emotional crack.

This could be triggered through a conversation that you have with someone that opens your heart. It could be through reading a poem. It could be through observing a beautiful sunset where you feel the grace of God and all the angels.

It is in those moments where our psyche experiences a crack, and we experience deep emotions. This is an extremely powerful and potent time to harvest the emotion in this moment and use the potency of the emotional experience to visualise and experience deeply your deepest heart's wishes fulfilled...

It is highly advisable to utilise this moment to send codes and frequencies into the quantum field, informing it that you have aligned with your heart's desires on a frequency level.

I have found this to be an extraordinary manifestation hack because there are so many times throughout our day and our week when we have these spontaneous emotional experiences, and it would serve us all well to remember to utilise these moments and harvest the crack in our emotional matrix, in order to turbo boost the quantum field with our matched intentional frequency.

I've discovered that accessing the quantum field via the imaginal faculties is extremely powerful, but if we can incorporate the emotional realm in our manifestation practice, this activates the manifestation process as if it is on steroids.

There are so many opportunities that we align with on a day-to-day level that open our hearts and enable us to feel the grace of the divine. These are the moments that I would deeply encourage you to work with, in order to send forth your pure heart's intentions into the quantum field.

When we work in this manner with quantum manifestation techniques, we experience a profound decrease in resistance, as the emotions literally carry the frequency of a golden cloud into the quantum field, informing the quantum field that we truly are a vibrational match to experience our hearts desires.

This is such an extraordinary, powerful, and potent way to work with the quantum field. I highly recommend that you take this protocol on board and apply it to your life asap.

"Life's battles don't always go to the stronger or faster man, But sooner or later the man who wins, is the man who thinks he can"

—NAPOLEON HILL

CHAPTER 19

FAITH IS A CHOICE

Faith is not something that comes naturally to us in the third dimension, as it requires us to place our belief in the unseen realm, which is something that we have definitely not been programmed to do.

But faith is Kryptonite to your heart's desires.

It is very important that we hold the vision and the feeling of that which we wish to experience consistently, and if we experience counter beliefs to this, it is very important that we write out these limiting beliefs and purge them in whatever way we deem appropriate.

Sacred Exercise

Please take out a sheet of paper and write out your limiting beliefs.

And then on another sheet of paper, write out the opposite, the antidote.

For example, if my limiting belief is, "Everyone always gets chosen and I don't" I would create an antidote belief that says, "I always get chosen by my soulmates". "I'm always chosen by the right people". "Everything that I wish to experience happens for me."

I would create an antidote to that limiting belief. And then I would write out the antidote on a separate piece of paper and sleep with it under my pillow and ask my subconscious mind to receive that new programming.

Top Manifesting Tip

It is very important that when we are focusing on manifesting our hearts desires that we act as if that which we are calling in has already manifested. For example, if you are manifesting the love of your life, then is your bedroom prepared? Is there space in your wardrobe? Is there a place on the kitchen table for your beloved to sit?

You need to show up and act as if that which you are aligning with has already manifested in your reality.

Sacred Exercise

Please take a moment now to make an inventory of all the manifestation techniques that you've used in your life that have worked for you. Write out everything that has worked that has created tangible measurable results for you.

CHAPTER 20

THE CURRENT WORLD SITUATION

There is so much going on in our world at the moment.

There's a huge battle between darkness and light. And if you look at what's going on in the world, you will see that the darkness is precipitating much light.

And by that, I mean that the more power and control the old controllers try to harness from humanity, the more humanity wakes up and unifies, and comes together to stand for sovereignty and freedom.

This is the vibration of profound light, which is precipitated from all of the darkness and contractions that the old controllers have been wishing to impose on humanity in this year of 2021.

I hope this clarifies the precipitation process of manifestation for you, and I hope that this understanding enables you to comprehend in layman's terms how the manifestation process truly works.

You are a master manifestor. You are highly adept at manifesting all your hearts desires from the quantum field into your third-dimensional reality.

You have absolutely every single thing that you need within you to manifest every single one of your heart's desires and your DNA is coded for success.

This is my deepest intention that you take all the faith in the universe from this chapter, and you apply it to your own hearts consciousness to know and remember who you truly are.

You are God's daughter, you are God's son, and as such there is no higher spiritual authority in the universe than you.

"There is no matter as such. All matter originates and exists only by virtue of a force which brings the particles of an atom to a vibration and holds this most minute solar system of the atom together. We must assume that behind this force is the existence of a conscious and intelligent mind. This mind is the matrix of all matter."

—MAX PLANCK

CHAPTER 21

THE FORTIFICATION PROCESS

As I come to the end of the journey of creating this manifestation manual and the accompanying light oracle deck, there are many aspects of the manifestation process that I have had the opportunity to meditate on.

In the last few days, I have been contemplating very deeply on the process of fortification and how manifestation is connected to the fortification process.

When we become aware of a holy desire that exists in our heart, and we understand that it already exists in the quantum field, and we remember that we are always connected to the quantum field via a string that connects us specifically to the manifestation of our heart's desires in the higher dimensional realms. Once we understand this, it is then a process of solidifying that which is somewhat etheric which exists in the quantum realm, to something that is tangible and solid that exists in the lower dimensional realms.

This is the fortification process.

In order to apply the fortification process, again, we come down to the incredibly important aspect of manifestation, which is consistency. In order to transform a heart desire from the higher dimensional realms into the third dimensional realm, we must consistently imprint upon our subconscious mind the fact that, that which we wish to experience has already manifested.

Indeed, that is the whole entire point of the manifestation process.

Our entire reality structure is based upon our perception of a holographic fractalled version of reality based upon our pineal gland's level of healing and clarity, and, therefore, it is always important to remember that it is what we see and what we perceive which is shaping and creating our version of reality in every single moment.

The truth of the matter is Mother-Father God, the universe, all that is, that which has a million names and that which is only one, gives each and every one of us a blank canvas in every single moment.

Every single moment we are given the opportunity to be a creator and imprint upon our subconscious mind the reality which we have come forth to experience. Therefore, the fortification process can be very much linked to the notion of imprinting upon our subconscious mind the fact that we are already experiencing that which we know exists in the quantum field on a higher dimensional realm of consciousness.

It is very important that we all meditate deeply on the ways that we can imprint our subconscious mind with this knowledge.

In this sacred manual, we have shared many examples and many sacred tools, but, of course, this is just the start. There are an infinite number of ways that we can work exceptionally proficiently with manifesting in the quantum field and, indeed, with the process of imprinting upon our subconscious mind the fact that our heart's desires have, indeed, already manifested right before our very eyes.

May you take inspiration from these words and may you meditate deeply on the fortification process and understand why consistency is so extremely important.

Another important aspect of the fortification process, of course, is faith. We will achieve nothing on our manifestation trajectory without faith. In fact, faith is the fire that transforms the structure of our heart's desire from the unseen realm and brings it forth into the seen realm. Faith is the furnace that enables our heart's desire to, literally, form in the lower dimensional realms of consciousness.

Of course, we must heal all the trauma that we have around faith, and we must atone all the timelines whereby our faith in God has been deeply challenged through betrayal and persecution.

This is our responsibility, and the awakened soul understands their duty to commit avidly to timeline recorrection work, whereby we, as our future self, go to the timeline whereby the trauma was experienced and we, literally, change the script, and we change the cellular memory in our genealogy and psyche.

This is because the subconscious mind does not know the difference between that which is imagined and that which is real.

Other aspects that enable the fortification process are:

- Acting as if that which we are manifesting has already happened,
- Preparing our physical space for our manifestations,
- Going about our day in the vibration that it has already manifest,
- Moving our physical world to create a space for that which we are manifesting.

For example, if we are manifesting a new car, we must clear the garage and clear the drive to hold the car. We must be prepared in many, many ways.

This is just one example of how we can deeply, deeply empower the fortification process.

One more way that we can empower the fortification process is remembering to maintain an extremely high and impeccable vibration, understanding that it is only our matrix programming that is keeping us stuck in a lower vibration.

When we train ourselves to go on rampages of gratitude and commit to a spiritual practice, we very quickly find that we naturally hold a high and buoyant vibration. The higher our vibration, the less interference we implement into the psychic field, enabling the fortification of our heart's desires to manifest with zero resistance.

This is such a huge subject matter, and I really pray that, this has been transmitted proficiently within this book. I will say one more thing about the fortification process for you all to ponder on.

You are the master of your destiny and you experience your destiny through the choices that you make. You can choose to indulge in thoughts of worry, fear, negativity and doubt, or you can choose to focus on counting your blessings and being a source of upliftment and positivity in the world.

No one is judging you. This is between you and you, you and your God self, you and your higher self. Your evolution is between you and the divine, no one else and nothing else, and evolution has never, ever been a competition.

If you choose to make choices that keep you in a low vibration, you will keep doing so until you say enough is enough, and you put down the mantle of victim consciousness and realise once and for all that Mother-Father God is a great and good God and has given you a blank and empty canvas in each and every moment so that you may create the precise and exact life of your dreams.

CHAPTER 22

VISUALISATION

I would like to spend a few paragraphs now, speaking about visualisation.

It is very important that we all understand that our imagination is directly linked to the imagination of God. We are all fractals of the one eternal divine essence of creation, and as such, we all hold a spark of that infinity within our own consciousness.

The whole entire fabric of creation is based upon a thought which is activated and implemented within the etheric blueprint level.

The etheric blueprint level is the foundation of the physical world, and we all have an implicit and direct relationship with this fundamental aspect of creation as such that whenever we visualise something, we are in effect, commanding its manifestation and we are pulling it out of the unseen realm, (the realm of infinite potential) into the realm of actuality and physicality.

This is how the whole of physical reality is constructed, and we each are endowed with full creative capabilities and capacities to be able to be the most extraordinary master manifestors.

There is nothing that you have to do to be able to imprint upon the unseen realm, your heart's desire.

Every child of God has been endowed with this eternal blessing and spiritual gift.

It is very important that you understand that absolutely everything in creation was created from a thought. And this is how we have constructed the reality that we are living in.

A light bulb was a thought in Edison's mind.

The airplane was a thought in the Wright brother's mind.

Absolutely everything in our physical reality started off as a thought, as something which was imagined, therefore it would serve you well to deeply honour and respect your imaginal faculties and understand the incredible auspicious power that you have at your fingertips, to be able to literally pull out of the unseen realm whatever your heart desires to manifest and experience in the physical.

We are all multi-dimensional Avatar souls, galactic beings that have existed, in many cases, since the big bang.

We all derive from eternal oneness into a fractaled experience of duality, but this is an illusion and is temporary and is masking the fact that we are all intimately and intricately connected as one.

The matrix has had everyone believe that they are a singular drop of water from the ocean, isolated, abandoned, alone with no sense of belonging in the universe, but the truth is you are the whole entire ocean.

That is the very definition of enlightenment, when one awakens from the illusion of being a separate drop of water, to the remembrance of the truth that I am the whole entire ocean.

May you remember this, may you take great power from these words that are reminding you of your true and eternal spiritual heritage.

You are an infinitely powerful creator, and you hold the most extraordinary technology in the universe to be able to manifest out of thin air everything and anything that your heart desires and you do this based purely through the imaginal faculties and through the focused visualisation and fortification process of holding faith while your manifestation is actualising from the unseen realm into the realm of physicality.

It is my deepest prayer that you take great power and inspiration from these words, and you own this transmission as if it is your own. There is no more time for waiting.

We are the ones that we have been waiting for and praying for.

The time is now for you to step up and remember who you are.

CHAPTER 23

COLLAPSING TIME

I would like to now devote the next few paragraphs to speaking about a very potent and little spoken aspect of the manifestation process.

In the creation of this book, I have opened and expanded my consciousness to receive new information and new codes that will deeply benefit the collective and enhance everybody's experience of manifestation, whoever has been blessed to read these sacred words.

I have been pondering very deeply about the notion of time, and it is my understanding that when we are calibrated to the third-dimensional dualistic linear time matrix, we step out of the zero-point field. The zero-point field is the present moment, where all past, present, and future timelines converge into the present moment of now.

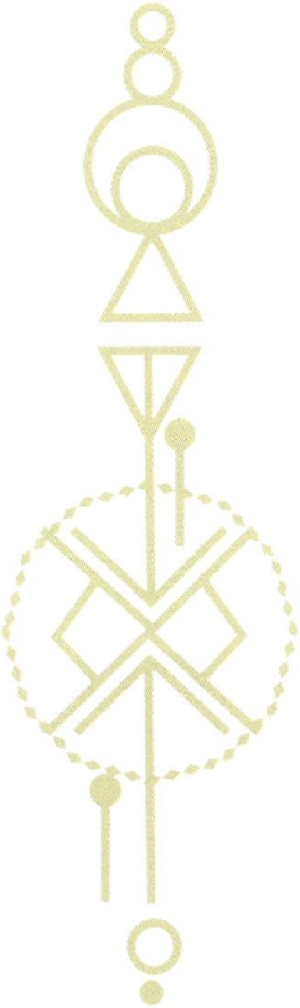

When we are identified with time and lock into questions, such as – "When?" and "How something is going to manifest?" We immediately take ourselves out of the zero-point field. And essentially, we take ourselves out of the fifth-dimensional Christ consciousness, frequency band, back down into the third-dimensional dualistic frequency band.

It is very important on the path of manifestation mastery that we transcend the time matrix and understand that the concept of linear time was created by the old controllers to keep us locked into illusion and in separation from our true Avatar Angelic consciousness that resides in the eternal zero-point moment of now.

In order to become a proficient manifester, I highly recommend that you understand that time is not linear. Time is elastic. Time is vertical. All timelines operate concurrently within the present moment of now, and wherever you, the Divine Avatar soul places your attention and intention, is the timeline experience that you will have.

So therefore, in order to become a proficient manifester, we have to step into the zero-point field, and we have to let go of all notions of waiting for something, or questioning how something is going to manifest.

And we must also let go of our deep addiction to perceiving our manifestation, and the manifestation process from a linear dualistic perspective.

Whenever we enter into the linear dualistic perspective around our manifestations, we disempower our creative quantum manifestation powers. They are exponentially diminished as we step out of the frequency of our true Avatar self into our egoic identity, which is anchored in illusion and limitation.

So therefore, in order to manifest proficiently, it is highly advisable that you enter into the zero-point field of consciousness. Understanding that the present moment is the culmination point of the souls searching and seeking.

The third-dimensional matrix has had everyone believe that we are searching for something external, such as a guru, a relationship, a training, a certificate, but the truth is we are searching for the experience of our consciousness arriving home and fully landing in the present moment of now.

When that happens, we understand that we hold an exceptionally powerful, creative potential to focus our attention and intention on the timeline that we wish to manifest.

Therefore, in order to become a proficient manifester, we collapse time in the sense that we collapse the questioning around how, when, where, or whereabouts, something is going to manifest as we understand that asking these questions keeps us trapped into a third-dimensional dualistic time matrix. Instead, we act as if that which we are manifesting has already arrived in our physical reality.

We match the frequency of our deepest heart's desires by showing up in the world as she, who is already experiencing that which we wish to manifest.

This is how we collapse time. We understand that in the zero-point field, that which we wish to manifest has already manifested. And so, we show up in that vibration.

This is what it means to collapse time and enter the zero-point field of manifestation mastery.

IN SUMMARY

As part of the concluding of this sacred manual, I would like to include a few paragraphs to share some extremely powerful and life changing tips that will enable you to maintain and hold a high spiritual frequency, which, as we know, is an essential part of being able to manifest our heart's desires.

Top Manifesting Tips

- I highly recommend becoming addicted to gratitude.
- Always remember to take actions on your desires and do not just sit there visualising.
- It is very important that we embrace and accept our shadow aspect and hunt for our shadow and be grateful when our shadow aspect gets triggered.
- We must remember that authenticity and transparency is one of the most potent ways to magnetise our spiritual destiny.
- Radical forgiveness is an extremely potent way to become a master manifestor.
- It is very much highly recommended that you have a high vibrational organic diet.
- I highly recommend bathing in spring water as spring water is the closest molecular structure that we have to living light. When we bathe in spring water, we are essentially bathing in light.
- Stay up to date with your vitamins, especially vitamin D.
- Dancing is an extremely powerful way to raise your frequency.
- A regular meditation practice is also highly recommended to maintain a high frequency.

- Find a spiritual community who welcomes you and celebrates you - being seen and heard and loved unconditionally by others is an extremely potent way to maintain a high spiritual frequency.
- Trust in God, your higher self, your I am presence, and know that you are never, ever a victim. Everything has been curated by you in order to bring you most efficiently to your enlightenment.
- Radical self-love. Knowing the universe loves you. Stand in the vibration of knowing that you are deeply loved by our Creator, Mother, Father, God.
- Never abandon yourself emotionally. Remember that if you abandon yourself emotionally, that is the mirror that you will create for all your relationships.
- Run towards yourself, run towards your shadow self and stand underneath all aspects of yourself and bring them home to the present moment.
- Bravery, courage and honest communication are extremely powerful modalities that will enable you to maintain a high vibration.
- Always remember that you are never, ever a victim and your life is a reflection of the choices that you make. You are empowered in every moment to change your directions and change your choices. This in turn will change your destiny.
- Heal all issues of self-worth and shame. It is very important that you identify any shame that you may be carrying. Shame is a powerful energy that can suppress the manifestation of our heart's desires and clearing shame is highly recommended.
- Ancestral clearing. Understand that you have taken on patterns via your ancestral lineage and if you are the awakened one in your lineage, you will have made a soul contract to stop the perpetuation of your ancestral patterning.

- Reprogram yourself to deeply remember that you are deserving of love. Understand that our mind is very open to hypnosis, the old false matrix is trying desperately to overwhelm our consciousness with its nefarious hypnotisms. This bullet point is a reminder to you that you can take charge of your own consciousness and hypnotise yourself to believing in the truth that you are a divine child of God and you are deeply deserving of love.

- Say thank you to your blessings, large and small. Always bless everything that comes into your path. Remember, that as a divine fractal of God, to experience lack is an extremely auspicious blessing. So, when you have outgrown evolving through lack, it is very important that you send an affirmation of blessing to your higher-self, informing your higher-self that you are complete with this lesson.

- Saying thank you to our fears and bodily symptoms is a game changer. When we know and remember that they are messengers from our emotional brain and are here to serve us, is the fast track to dissolving all symptoms...

It is very important that we understand that any physical symptoms that we have are messages from our nervous system, informing us that there are beliefs that are not in alignment with the will of our divine self.

There are many other bullet points that we could add to this list, and this is by no means a complete list.

Please feel free to meditate on all the ways that you can adopt in order to maintain an extremely impeccable and high frequency, so that you may become the master manifestor that Mother, Father, God created you to be through hacking the quantum field.

"Einstein proved that everything in the universe is energy. All energy vibrates at particular frequencies. We are energy too and so each of us is also vibrating at a frequency. Your thoughts, feelings and beliefs determine the vibration and frequency of your energy."

—RHONDA BYRNE

CONCLUSION

What an extremely powerful journey this has been, bringing through this sacred manifestation mastery manual.

I have shared with you my deepest soul truth, and the deepest and most potent manifestation hacks that I have encountered in my 25 years of being profoundly committed to becoming a master manifestor.

Please understand, this is not an exhaustive list, and please feel free to write to me at my email address of ***cosmicgypsy33@gmail.com*** to share with me your most potent manifestation hacks.

I will do a second edition in the next few months, sharing my communities' most potent manifestation hacks.

It is very important that everyone reading these words understands and remembers who you are.

You are a child of God, you are in direct alignment to receive the inheritance of the Kingdom and Queendom of Mother-Father, God.

The third-dimensional matrix has sought to impose a lie upon you of your true origins and your true spiritual power.

It is your duty to awaken from the heinous programming that has been enforced upon you, divine precious child of God.

You are your own saviour.

There is no external saviour other than yourself.

You are the one that bought into the lies and the programming, and it is only you and your consciousness that can free yourself from the old belief structure.

"Imagination is more important than Knowledge"

—A.EINSTEIN

PLEASE LEAVE A REVIEW FOR MANIFESTATION MASTERY ON AMAZON

It is my deepest and sincere prayer that this book has given you a profound understanding of manifestation mastery and I hope you will find this book to be a valuable resource.

If you have enjoyed this book and found it helpful, please consider leaving a review on Amazon. Your reviews are hugely helpful to me as a published author and will help others be able to find this book in the Amazon search results.

MANIFESTATION MASTERY BOOK REVIEWS

"We are living in a very fearful world. Jen McCarty's "Manifestation Mastery" -How To Work With The Quantum Field and Hack The Matrix - is the book you must absolutely read in times like this.

Currently, it's seeming, we are living in two worlds, the in-between material world, and the spiritual world. The planet itself is shedding old systems, yet our human nature is still not realizing the shift of consciousness and is keeping our mind in the old world. That make it so confusing and make us all very fearful. Although the whole universe is supporting us and continues to raise our frequency -, shedding old systems down and trying to wake us up, but the fear of the unknown makes us uneasy.

Jen's step by step spiritual teaching is tremendously help for our spiritual awakening experience. Her 25 years of loving and gentle teachings are absolutely sinking into our soul. I have read the first three chapters of her book today and the flow of topics are so deep and widely covered whilst also covering the whole process needed to create a solid spiritual practice. Her writing itself raises my vibration and I feel like her every word replaces and upgrades my sub-consciousness with new light codes. I truly believe that this activation is helping and opening a new doorway of my life path.

Thank you so much Jen for your tirelessness work to unite our soul families and to keep pushing us moving ahead without fear. Your book was so beautifully written. Highly recommended for people on all stages of their spiritual journey. My heart continues to keep singing after reading your book. I can't wait to read the rest of the book upon launch. Thank you again! Namaste" – ***Yukari***

"Dearest Jen

Wow it's such an honour to be part if your street team and get to read the first few chapters of this Manifestation Masterpiece. The words echo beyond in the quantum realm, and I can literally see my future self in all this abundance and health and wealth.

This is a gift to humanity, reminding us of our sacred dreams and desires. Thank you." - ***Lulila R***

"Wow another masterpiece…

Every word Jen writes brings a remembrance of oneness and arriving back into the present moment.

Just from reading these first 3 chapters has enabled me to alchemise unwanted thought patterns and arrive back to the zero point of heart centred stillness.

Remembering that all of our desires are sacred and that we are worthy of receiving everything our heart desires and that it is our birth right to have.

It truly is by arriving at our destination/desires first that we received, and we do this by residing in our hearts and feeling grateful for already having our manifestation.

This will be my go-to book every time I feel myself slipping back into unwanted thoughts of lack, thank you Jen I beyond grateful for your channelling's." **Sally F.**

Jen's book, Manifestation Mastery, is an absolutely wonderful tool to use to achieve all your heart's desires and hack the matrix. Jen breaks it all down in an easy read format that anyone can understand. It is a powerful journey so, be prepared for drastic changes in your life. Showing up and being consistent is key. Since working with Jen's techniques I am ready to manifest a beautiful life. **Corrine H.**

MANIFESTATION MASTERY NOW AVAILABLE AS AN AUDIOBOOK

Purchase Manifestation Mastery Audiobook Here - Jens' Website

https://jenmccarty.co.uk/audiobooks/

It is very powerful to receive the audio version as there is an opportunity to receive my words and my voice. Our voice is a reflection of our soul signature and enables us to very deeply connect with the soul frequency of the person that is sharing.

TWIN FLAMES AND THE EVENT

A MESSAGE FOR THE 144,000 LIGHTWORKERS

- What is a Twin Flame?
- Does everyone have a Twin Flame?

- How do I meet my Twin Flame?
- Why are Twin Flames such a hot topic at the moment?
- And what do Twin Flames have to do with the Great Awakening that we are experiencing as a collective?

Billions of books have been created in the world, and you were drawn to this book for a reason. Your higher self has brought you to this book, and this is because it contains codes that are specifically connected to you and your evolutionary journey towards spiritual mastery and eternal union with your Twin Flame.

Purchase Twin Flames and The Event Paperback Here - Amazon

TWIN FLAMES AND THE EVENT BOOK REVIEWS

"After a lifelong struggle of working to overcome the effects of extreme abuse in my childhood, I have arrived at perhaps the most challenging period of my life, facing PTSD, flashback after flashback, and just so much pain. I write this now because I want to say that this book, TWIN FLAMES AND THE EVENT, has come to me in the midst of this processing. I didn't know if I could even concentrate on the book, each line, or each word. But guidance said, "Read, even just one sentence for now." So I did! As I read, starting from the very first word of the prologue, I felt hope coming back! I felt God within me warm my heart and fill my soul! I felt the remembrance and knowing of the truth in each line; that even in the chaos of all of this that I am experiencing, I am "the lighthouse" that I had once promised that I would be. I had felt so mired in my life circumstances (have also experienced chronic illness for 20+ years), that I had felt my faith slipping away. Yet, as I read Jen McCarty's words, "It is absolutely and purely about faith," I felt the living, loving, Divine frequencies encoded in these words! My heart embraced them and enveloped them very peacefully and

lovingly! It's really quite challenging to describe the experience of reading this incredible book! Jen was not kidding when she said, "In this book, every word is specifically directed to support you to very swiftly align with the Spiritual master-avatar being that you truly are - the galactic, angelic, timeless, off-spring of eternal love." I am writing about just a small portion of these beautiful, sacred, holy gifts that are encoded energetically in each and every word! There is just so much to say about this book that I could go on for quite some time. Suffice it to say that over the past 20+ years of my spiritual journey, I have purchased countless good books, but I honestly feel that this one is superior to all of those. Jen McCarty has channeled a book like no other! Once I started my "one sentence" in which I had been guided, I did not want to stop. Not only is this book filled with ancient wisdom, it is a dynamic Divine experience. I know that I will read and re-read this many times, as I have already started my second reading. Immense gratitude, Jen McCarty! This book will change countless lives! I know it's changing mine! Transformative, Beautiful, , Relatable, Divine! What a gift!" ***Jill***

"Twin flames and the event" is a rare gem of a book. Within minutes of reading I had received such great insight that I literally had to take time out to reassess my life. I was then able to reframe past life events in such a way that I felt enormous relief and sense of peace as I realised that everything in my life had in fact played out to perfection. After this realisation I was straight back into the book, for it is extremely compelling as there is a plethora of information. Jen McCarty writes as an authority on the subject of twin flames, which is a very hot topic at the moment. But Jen has been interested in this field since her awakening in 1995 but has waited until this time to put her knowledge into a book for the general public. For it is now perfect timing: the book was released in the first season of Aquarius after the planet's shift into the age of Aquarius at the last equinox. Thus, Jen is writing at the cutting edge of time, as it is only now that her information could be received. It is then no surprise that this is no ordinary book, for it is infused with energetic codes to trigger remembrances and awakenings. As such it is one of a kind and I cannot wait to receive Jen's next offering." ***Kate***

TWIN FLAMES AND THE EVENT WORKBOOK AND MP3 ACTIVATIONS

Jen has written a workbook which is the perfect companion for the sacred text – Twin Flames And The Event.

Halfway through writing Twin Flames and The Event – I was very strongly guided by spirit to create a workbook that would accompany this powerful sacred scripture. So therefore, I followed this guidance and brought through an amazing offering that will assist you to deeply and understand and assimilate all of the information and codes that are shared in the book.

I would highly recommend everybody work with the workbook, as the exercises and MP3 activations work on a deeply subconscious level and work with the incredible power of symbols, which are **the** language of the unconscious mind.

If you really want to experience a shift in your vibrational reality and receive great assistance in truly becoming one with your higher self, then I highly recommend you gift yourself this beautiful workbook that goes alongside this sacred text.

Working with the MP3 activations which accompany the workbook deeply and profoundly fast tracks your spiritual ascension path and enables you to activate these codes of transformation very swiftly and efficiently within your energetic system. I cannot recommend working with these activations highly enough.

Purchase Twin Flames and The Event eWorkbook and MP3 Activations Here - Jens Website

https://jenmccarty.co.uk/workbooks/

Purchase Twin Flames and The Event Paperback Workbook Here - Amazon

https://www.amazon.co.uk/Twin-Flames-Event-Message-Lightworkers/dp/1838394109/ref=sr_1_2?crid=1HRMEQ7K7BGOA&keywords=jen+mccarty&qid=1651561192&sprefix=jen+mccarty%2Caps%2C189&sr=8-2

NO MORE CRUMBS

AN EMPOWERMENT MANUAL FOR THE DIVINE FEMININE

Women all around the world have been programmed to accept crumbs. This has to end. Women are goddesses and need to transform their inner world to fully and completely accept this truth. As soon as a woman accepts that she is a goddess she collapses all old patterns pertaining to accepting crumbs and she co-creates brand-new subconscious patterns which support her to attract devotion from her pre-destined true love.

The world is changing before our eyes and never before has it been so important for Twin Flame / God mates to come together.

This book will help you to so deeply and profoundly release all programming around accepting crumbs in romantic relationships. It will transform your inner beliefs and subconscious mind and assist you to attract your true love with ease and grace and great swiftness.

NO MORE CRUMBS BOOK REVIEWS

AN EMPOWERMENT MANUAL FOR THE DIVINE FEMININE

"From the opening paragraph I felt held and lifted, an expansion of my heart and activity in my third eye. Part of me was shouting yes! I remember and the words flowed into my consciousness, being and belong there. As I read on, I recognised the truth of your words and the patterns of my relationships and here was guidance to co-create the reality of my desire. The wisdom shared illuminated a reinterpretation of events and a deeper understanding of who I, we are. This book is a compass for all feminines' to step into their power and navigate their lives. Thank you is insufficient for such an amazing gift of guidance." ***Namaste, Karen***

"I have read the first five chapters of your amazing book "No More Crumbs" and I was flabbergasted at how much this book resonated with my healing journey. After I had read the chapters I experienced many activations and synchronicities start to manifest in my life. I was able to capture all of the red flags I have overlooked due to the conditioning and programming. I immediately stopped tolerating standoffish behaviour from men. I started to manifest getting a new tribe of nice, fun and genuine people to hang out with. I even got two interviews for two jobs which I had recently applied for. I am so humbled at this opportunity you have given me Jen. it will be an honour to buy and read the whole book and apply it to my life." ***Lisseth***

NO MORE CRUMBS WORKBOOK AND MP3 ACTIVATIONS

Working with the MP3 activations which accompany the No More Crumbs Workbook deeply and profoundly fast tracks your spiritual ascension path and enables you to activate these codes of transformation very swiftly and efficiently within your energetic system. I cannot recommend working with these activations highly enough.

Purchase No More Crumbs eWorkbook and MP3 Activations Here - Jens Website

https://jenmccarty.co.uk/product-category/no-more-crumbs/workbook-meditations/

Purchase No More Crumbs Paperback Workbook Here – Amazon

https://www.amazon.co.uk/No-More-Crumbs-Empowerment-Feminine/dp/B099TL62FG/ref=tmm_pap_swatch_0?_encoding=UTF8&qid=&sr=

AUDIOBOOKS

Please know that I have bought through the audio versions of my books Twin Flames & The Event and No More Crumbs.

It is very powerful to receive the audio version as there is an opportunity to receive my words and my voice. Our voice is a reflection of our soul signature and enables us to very deeply connect with the soul frequency of the person that is sharing.

TWIN FLAMES AND THE EVENT

AUDIOBOOK REVIEWS

"Thank you, Jen! I loved the hard copy version, but I love the audio even more!

There is something about Jen's voice and the messages that she brings forth that connects deeply with my inner knowing. I know I will listen back many, many, many times." ***Jade W.***

"THANK YOU. Your beautiful soul radiates brilliantly & inspires so greatly. My gratitude for You & Your resilient strength is immeasurable. Namaste." – ***April***

"So deeply profound and enlightening. This book has brought me to a wonderfully heightened state of awareness and has prompted me to want more from the author." – ***Anon***

Purchase Twin Flames and The Event Audiobook Here – Jens' Website

https://jenmccarty.co.uk/audiobooks/

Purchase Twin Flames and The Event Audiobook Here - Audible

https://www.amazon.co.uk/Twin-Flames-Event-Message-Lightworkers/dp/B094PV2F2F/ref=tmm_aud_swatch_0?_encoding=UTF8&qid=&sr=

Purchase No More Crumbs Audiobook Here - Jens' Website

https://www.amazon.co.uk/No-More-Crumbs-Empowerment-Feminine/dp/B09TN48ZZV/ref=tmm_abk_swatch_0?_encoding=UTF8&qid=&sr=

Purchase No More Crumbs Audiobook Here - Audible

PLEASE LEAVE A REVIEW ON AUDIBLE

If you have enjoyed listening to any of my audiobooks, please consider leaving a review on Audible. Your reviews are hugely helpful to me as a published author and will help others be able to find my audiobooks in the Audible search results.

LAW OF ATTRACTION

LITTLE INSTRUCTION BOOK

The book consists of an introduction whereby I share with you all my downloads about how to work very deeply and powerfully with the law of attraction and the rest of the book is a combination of quotes and affirmations from well-known people that have worked successfully with the law of attraction.

This is a book of miracles, a tale of timeless truth and a promise to the most ancient part of ourselves to remember and align with the highest vibration of who we are.

LAW OF ATTRACTION LITTLE INSTRUCTION BOOK

BOOK REVIEW

"Absolutely awesome book just as you would expect from Jen She really is a beautiful being of light with a heart that desires everyone else's light to shine. Thank you Jen." ***Carla.***

Purchase Law of Attraction - Little Instruction Book Paperback Here - Amazon

https://www.amazon.co.uk/Law-Attraction-Little-Instruction-Book/dp/B08WK2LGZY/ref=sr_1_3?crid=1Y6K-5BRO4RXM3&keywords=jen+mccarty+books+law+of+attraction&qid=1651561484&s=books&sprefix=jen+mccarty+books+law+of+attraction%2Cstripbooks%2C76&sr=1-3

OVERVIEW OF JENS SACRED OFFERINGS

Jen is very excited to be branching out with her spiritual work in order to share the original and powerful modalities which her higher-self has shared with her.

She is offering regular live training throughout the year as well as many self-paced programs. These trainings and programs are packed with Ascension codes that will enable you to up level your spiritual vibration very quickly and very efficiently.

Jen is an extremely powerful facilitator, and it is highly recommended to sign up to the live trainings whereby you get close access to Jen. If you are unable to attend the live trainings, then we highly recommend working with the self-paced programs. Jen is continuously bringing through powerful life changing programs that will massively affect your spiritual vibration and enable you to stabilise in unity consciousness.

There are lots of different ways in which you can work with Jen; in her containers, in her facilitator trainings and with her MP3 activation programs.

Here is an overview of Jens' Sacred Offerings;

- Spiritual Containers – Live Online Trainings
- Monthly Global Transmissions and After Parties
- 21 Day DNA Activation Programs - Online Programs
- DNA Activation MP3 Series
- Books, Audiobooks, Workbooks and MP3 Meditations
- Jen has been inspired to create a brand-new Etsy shop filled with products that are infused with celestial and angelic light codes.

SPIRITUAL CONTAINERS – LIVE ONLINE TRAININGS

In the last few months Jen has been guided to host spiritual containers, she has hosted;

- Prosperity Unleashed
- Twin Flame
- Nervous System Recalibration
- Write and Publish your Book

The containers are an opportunity to go on an extremely powerful, deep, and intimate journey with Jen and a small group of participants to massively transform programming around wealth, love and belonging.

If you are interested in learning more about Jens spiritual containers, please feel free to email her assistant at ***info@jenmccarty.co.uk*** and she will send you all of the information regarding the upcoming containers.

SELF-PACED ONLINE PROGRAMS

Jen will also be creating a number of self-paced online programs that will be based upon the containers which will enable people to do the program without having to show up for the live calls. Please look out for all the information on Jen's powerful self-paced online programs on her website ***www.jenmccarty144.com.***

MONTHLY GLOBAL TRANSMISSIONS

Since 2016 Jen has been hosting regular global transmissions on numerological portal dates such as 2:2, 3:3, 4:4 etc. Also, on Pagan holidays such as Samhain Imbolc, Equinox and Solstice. The reason for this is that it is so important that the Awakened Star Crew gather together on powerful dates such as these, in order to align our will and intention, with the will and intention of Mother-Father God.

TRANSMISSION AFTER PARTIES

As well as hosting the transmissions Jen now hosts transmission after parties which happen directly after the transmission. This is an opportunity to come and spend close and intimate time with Jen and to go deeper into the codes that have been shared in the transmission. The transmission after party is proving extremely popular with Jens' community.

21 DAY DNA ACTIVATION PROGRAMS – ONLINE PROGRAMS

Jen has produced a number of 21-day DNA activation programs on;

- Attract 1 Million Followers
- Miracle Hair Growth
- EMF Protection
- Abundance
- Age Regeneration
- Divine Love

Each 21 Day Program comes with a meditation which is highly activating for your DNA plus an E-Book with exercises to follow during the 21 days.

It is highly advisable to work with a program for 21 days as it gives you enough time to take on a brand-new habit and it is our habits that ultimately change our life. I have been getting the most phenomenal feedback from all the people in my community that have been doing these programs and they are highly advisable if you wish to fast-track your spiritual evolution.

DNA ACTIVATION MP3 SERIES

In addition to the global transmissions, Jen has been guided by spirit to produce specific transmissions which address certain topics affecting the collective consciousness. This makes it much easier for people to be able to choose which area of their life they wish to work on to address their personal challenges. For example, reclaiming your self-worth and healing sexual trauma etc.

SPECIAL MP3 ACTIVATIONS

I also have two special activations; one is called the "Yoni Nidra" and the other is called "Miracle IBS Healing". These are long in-depth healing meditations that will massively affect your healing journey and spiritual vibration.

BOOKS / AUDIOBOOKS / WORKBOOKS AND MP3 ACTIVATIONS

- Jen is a published author of four books with more books soon to be published;
- Twin Flames and The Event – A Message for the 144,000 Lightworkers
- No More Crumbs – An Empowerment Manual for the Divine Feminine
- Law of Attraction – Little Instruction Book
- Manifestation Mastery – How to Work with the Quantum Field and Hack the Matrix – Plus the accompanying Oracle Deck is also due to be published soon.
- "Divine Actor - I Am" is also due to be published soon.

WORKBOOKS AND MP3 ACTIVATIONS

Twin Flames and The Event and No More Crumbs both have an accompanying workbook with exercises and DNA Activating MP3s which are perfect companions for these sacred texts and will assist you to deeply understand and assimilate all of the information and codes which are shared in the books.

Jen highly recommends everybody work with the workbooks, as the exercises and meditations work on a deeply subconscious level and work with the incredible power of symbols, which are the language of the unconscious mind.

AUDIOBOOKS

Please know that I have bought through the audio versions of my books Twin Flames and The Event and No More Crumbs. It is very powerful to receive the audio version as there is an opportunity to receive my words and my voice. Our voice is a reflection of our soul signature and enables us to very deeply connect with the soul frequency of the person that is sharing.

JEN IS NOW ON ETSY!

Jen has been inspired to create a brand-new Etsy shop filled with products that are infused with celestial and angelic light codes. There are beautiful and powerful products in her Etsy shop such as light-coded cushions, light-coded journals and cups - it is highly recommended that you check out her shop.

https://www.etsy.com/shop/jenmccarty144?ref=shop_sugg

ABOUT THE AUTHOR - JEN MCCARTY

Widely known as the healer of healers - Jen McCarty has earned the most astonishing place in everyone's heart. As a published author - Jen assists people with addiction recovery, as well as helping many people heal their core wounds on a soul level. Jen had a massive life-changing Kundalini Awakening when she was just 21, in the Himalayas in Northern India, chanting the mantra "Om Namah Shivaya". From that moment on she passed over the threshold from third-dimensional consciousness to fully stabilising in fifth-dimensional consciousness.

Jen has since devoted her whole adult life serving her brothers and sisters and has been blessed with a massive amount of extremely dedicated followers over the last 5 years and has built up a social media following of over 175,000 people.

Jen specialises in working with the reunion of Twin Flames and the removal of roadblocks that stand in the way of that. She is an awakened spiritual teacher, deeply and highly skilled at facilitating a space for all those who she comes into contact with. She has a phenomenal track record in uniting many, many Twin Flames, assisting them to connect with their multi-dimensional aspect and activating the Hieros Gamos – the inner alchemical marriage of the masculine and feminine energies within, and very skilfully identifying and removing all blocks that stand in the way of triumphant Twin Flame Union.

Jen has experienced huge breakthroughs recently due to working with very high-level mentors who are fully anchored in the millionaire mindset. This is having a huge impact on her working and her offerings that she has begun to share.

Visit Jen McCarty's Website Here

https://jenmccarty.co.uk/

JOIN JEN'S SACRED COMMUNITIES ON SOCIAL MEDIA

Cosmicgypsy33 - Jen McCarty - LINKTREE WEBLINKS

www.linktr.ee/cosmicgypsy33

Official Jen McCarty - INSTAGRAM

www.instagram.com/officialjenmccarty144/

Jen McCarty23 - FACEBOOK

www.facebook.com/jen.mccarty23/

The Event is Happening - FACEBOOK GROUP

www.facebook.com/groups/theeventishappening

Cosmic Gypsy - Jen McCarty - YOUTUBE

www.youtube.com/channel/UC_8fJz5gAnhRqZ740QXlzmw

The Event is Happening - TELEGRAM GROUP

www.t.me/Theeventishappening

JenJen144 - Jen McCarty - GAB

www.gab.com/jenjen144

Printed in Poland
by Amazon Fulfillment
Poland Sp. z o.o., Wrocław
07 November 2023

976b5ce3-45ff-485a-ab8d-665a25a24260R01